ENJOYING

GOD'S

MERCY

JOE-JESIMIEL OGBE

Enjoying God's Mercy

ISBN: 978-978-947-880-4

Published In Nigeria by

Young Disciples Press

3, YDI str, Off Isheri-LASU Rd, Hotel Bus Stop,

Igando-Lagos, Nigeria

01-2934286, 08023124455

www.ydiworld.org

joejesimiel2006@yahoo.com

AllScripture quotations are from the King James Version of the Bible, except otherwise stated.

Book Design & Printing In Nigeria:

Learnible

www.openlearnible.com

+234 8035215240

TABLE OF CONTENTS

Introduction

Each time I take a mental journey back to my yesteryears, and cogitate about the various stages of my life, I find God's mercy at work. I always see the influence, power and awesomeness of His mercy. I can candidly testify that it's been God's mercy all the way. I am who I am by His grace and mercy. What I am today is a function of His mercy; and what I will be tomorrow can only be by His mercy. I'm absolutely nothing outside of His mercy. I am a veritable vessel of His mercy!

As human beings, we are all dead in transgressions, iniquities and sins, hence the need for His mercy. His mercy restrained Him from dealing with us according to our sin. "He hath not dealt with us after our sins; nor rewarded us according to our iniquities."

(Ps. 103:10)

God's mercy has the power to treat us as freshers as if we had done no wrong. God's mercy is free and unmerited to all wrongdoers. If we have to do something grievous to ourselves in order to merit it, then it is no longer mercy. We don't have to perform some painful penances like cutting our bodies with sharp objects like prophets of Baal or going through fire all in a bid to merit His mercy. We don't have to expiate our wrong doings or transgressions to enjoy His mercy.

What wrong, sin or crime have you committed?

There is no sin or wrong beyond mercy! I don't care about the crime you have committed or the wrong you have done; what I care about is the fact that God who empowered a murderer in the person of Moses to serve His purpose in Egypt can use anybody to fulfill His agenda. God divinely decided to show Moses mercy by preserving his life, and empowering him to go deliver the children of Israel. Are you a murderer like Moses, reading this book? There is hope for you! God shall arise on your behalf to show you mercy. Are you a chronic liar, fornicator, womaniser or adulterer? There is hope for you! Are you a convicted criminal sentenced to death or serving life in prison? There is hope for you!

I pray and prophesy vehemently that God will show up on your behalf and you shall be set free! With the eyes of faith, I see you surrendering to the Lordship of Christ Jesus right now. I see Him forgiving and washing you clean from every sin that you have ever committed. And I also see God orchestrating the steps of a judge, a governor or your president with the prerogative of mercy coming to set you free today in Jesus name!

God is never shocked by your ordinariness or vulnerability. No! He knows you're human and He knows just how to motivate you not to give up no matter the challenges you are confronted with. He is a God of ordinary people. It is His mercy that makes anyone extraordinary. Joseph became great in Egypt because God showed him mercy. "But the LORD was with Joseph, and shewed him mercy, and gave him favour in the sight of the keeper of the prison."

(Genesis 39:21)

Show me one person in scriptures that was made great by his or her own power! None! The people we look up to and celebrate as God's veritable vessels were all ordinary individuals but God chose or located them; He empowered them and released them as products of His mercy to do awesome things.

Are you conscious of your own limitations, struggles and vulnerability? You have a choice. You can either give up by quarantining yourself to a life of self-pity and hopelessness or you can rise up like Jabez to call on the merciful God to change your status. Jabez was an ordinary person but God changed his story when he prayed. The Bible says, "And Jabez called on the God of Israel, saying, Oh that thou wouldest bless me indeed, and enlarge my coast, and that thine hand might be with me, and that thou wouldest keep me from evil, that it may not grieve me! And God granted him that which he requested." (1 Chro 4:10)

As a young Christian, I used to wonder why God did not save pop stars, prominent personalities and mighty individuals. I even used to pray for their salvation. My understanding then was that if God saved them, they could turn their fans to God. But I now know that God could not choose them for fear that they would glory in their own abilities, personalities and achievements. Their outstanding results can get in the way, preventing people from seeing God's mercy or power. They too may not see themselves as products of mercy or see the God factor in their achievements.

Haven't you seen the so called self-made individuals and celebrities glorying in their abilities or accomplishments? As Christians we cannot afford to glory in ourselves or our abilities. We can only glory in God! The Bible says, "For ye see your calling, brethren, how that not many wise men after the flesh, not many mighty, not many noble, are called: But

God hath chosen the foolish things of the world to confound the wise; and God hath chosen the weak things of the world to confound the things which are mighty; And base things of the world, and things which are despised, hath God chosen, yea, and things which are not, to bring to nought things that are: That no flesh should glory in his presence. But of him are ye in Christ Jesus, who of God is made unto us wisdom, and righteousness, and sanctification, and redemption: That, according as it is written, He that glorieth, let him glory in the Lord."

(1Cor 1:26-31)

Are there any laid down steps or procedures you must follow to provoke His mercy? How can you attract His mercy, if no self-punishment is required to atone for your sins? Beloved reader, I sincerely believe that God has inspired me to write this book to help answer these questions and other issues bothering many people on this vital subject of mercy. This book project is my attempt to show you that so many millions of people are beneficiaries of God's mercy. His mercy is inexhaustible! Billions have taken delivery of it, yet it is far from being exhausted! It is as fresh, as full, and as free as ever! His mercy is unfailing and everlasting. According to Spurgeon, C. H., "There is nothing little in God; His mercy is like Himself—it is infinite. You cannot measure it. His mercy is so great that it forgives great sins to great sinners, after great lengths of time, and then gives

5

great favours and great privileges, and raises us up to great enjoyments in the great heaven of the great God."

You too can enjoy or procure His mercy, if only you are willing to embrace knowledge. Yes, you can, if only you are willing to embrace the truths and instructions in this book. As you prayerfully read this inspiring book, I urge you to deliberately put your trust in the Lord wholly and completely. This is because it is by His mercy that you are stabilized. No force on earth is powerful enough to move you, even as you depend solely on His mercy! "For the king trusteth in the LORD, and through the mercy of the most High he shall not be moved."

(Psalms 21:7)

Joe-jesimiel Ogbe

October, 2016

Chapter One

WHAT IS MERCY?

Mercy is undeserved kindness and compassion.

Mercy is when it is within your power to punish or deal ruthlessly with someone but you decide out of a heart of compassion to forgive the person. In many countries of the world, there are leaders that have the prerogative of mercy. They have the power to forgive or pardon even convicted hardened criminals. They have the power to tamper justice with mercy!

Mercy is forgiveness! It takes mercy to forgive someone who has wronged you. Only a merciful heart can forgive others. Forgiveness procures forgiveness! You hold yourself back from enjoying the forgiveness of God if you refuse to forgive others. Forgive your fellow man and God will forgive you. That means you are the initiator of forgiveness. "For if ye forgive men their trespasses, your heavenly Father will also forgive you: But if ye forgive not men their trespasses, neither will your Father forgive your trespasses."

(Matthew 6:14-15)

God's mercy is so great that He doesn't just forgive your sins, but He goes ahead to erase any record of your sins. Someone said, "Mercy is about God not punishing us as our sins deserve, and grace is God blessing us despite the fact that we do not deserve it. Mercy is deliverance from judgment. Grace is extending kindness to the unworthy."

A plea to God for mercy is asking Him to withhold the judgment or punishment we deserve and instead grant to us the forgiveness we desperately need. Mercy is not earned! My beloved, none of us deserves anything from God. God does not owe us anything. Anything good that we experience is a result of the grace of God. Grace is simply defined as unmerited favour. God favours, or gives us good things that we do not deserve and could never earn. We are rescued from judgment by God's mercy.

God is the source of all mercies! He has the capacity to grant you mercy before men and women. He has the capacity to turn the heart of man to be favourably disposed toward you. "The king's heart is in the hand of the LORD, as the rivers of water: he turneth it whithersoever he will." (Pro 21:1)

It's only by His great mercy that He did not allow the enemy to destroy or put an end to your life.

The truth is that if not for His mercies we all would have been consumed. The Bible says, "It is of the LORD'S mercies that we are not consumed, because his compassions fail not. They are new every morning: great is thy faithfulness." (Lam 3:22-23)

Enjoying the mercy of God is a possibility because God is a merciful God! Procuring God's mercy is possible because God is rich in mercy. If God were to deal with us according to our shortcomings and sins, we would all be condemned for eternity. David cries out, "Have mercy upon me, O God, according to thy lovingkindness: according unto the multitude of thy tender mercies blot out my transgressions. Wash me throughly from mine iniquity, and cleanse me from my sin." (Ps 51:1-2)

Without His mercy, our sins or transgressions would still be hurting us. His mercy makes Him to forgive and blot out our transgressions. His mercy makes Him to wash away all our iniquities and to cleanse us from all unrighteousness. God is competent to be merciful because He is utterly and competently self-sufficient in Himself.

Mercy is a quality intrinsic to the nature of God. The devil does not possess this quality, hence he or his cohorts can never show mercy. Only God and His true sons and daughters have the capacity to show mercy. The Bible says, "And his servants said unto him, Behold now, we have heard that the kings of the house of Israel are merciful kings: let us, I pray thee, put sackcloth on our loins, and ropes upon our heads, and go out to the king of Israel: peradventure he will save thy life." (1 Kings 20:31)

David understood this mercy-quality about God and chose to fall into the hands of God instead of man! "And David said unto Gad, I am in a great strait: let us fall now into the hand of the LORD; for his mercies are great: and let me not fall into the hand of man." (2 Sam 24:14)

God's mercy is a driving force in causing Him not to forsake us, destroy us and forget His covenant promises. The Bible says, "For the LORD thy God is a merciful God; he will not forsake thee, neither destroy thee, nor forget the covenant of thy fathers which he sware unto them." (Deut 4:31)

Salvation is a validation of mercy and grace of God! By His mercy humanity can gain access to salvation. Jesus Christ is salvation personified! If we receive Him as Saviour, we receive mercy from God and we are delivered from judgment. Instead of judgment, we receive by grace, salvation, forgiveness of sins, and an eternity with Him in Heaven, the most wonderful place imaginable.

How do we secure God's riches or blessings? It is simply by boldly and confidently approaching the throne of grace so that we may receive mercy and find grace to help us in our time of need. The mercy of God is obtainable! The Bible says, "Let us therefore come boldly unto the throne of grace, that we may obtain mercy, and find grace to help in time of need." (Hebrews 4:16)

God being merciful basically means that, when we deserve punishment, He doesn't punish us. Mercy is the withholding of a just condemnation or punishment. God's mercy is about His kindness to man! Just as David showed kindness to Mephibosheth, God is more than prepared and willing to show us kindness because of His Son, Jesus Christ. "And David said unto him, Fear not: for I will surely shew thee kindness for Jonathan thy father's sake, and will restore thee all the land of Saul thy father; and thou shalt eat bread at my table continually." (2 Samuel 9:7)

Jesus gave a powerful parable to illustrate God's mercy. "Therefore is the kingdom of heaven likened unto a certain king, which would take account of his servants. And when he had begun to reckon, one was brought unto him, which owed him ten thousand talents. But forasmuch as he had not to pay, his lord commanded him to be sold, and his wife, and children, and all that he had, and payment to be made. The servant therefore fell down, and worshipped him, saying, Lord, have patience with me, and I will pay thee all. Then the lord of that servant was moved with compassion, and loosed him, and forgave him the debt." (Mat 18:23-27)

God, like the king in this passage forgives anyone who truly begs Him for mercy. Just as the debtor came and begged for mercy, you too can ask God to forgive you. The vital point is that you and I owed God a debt which we could never repay, but God in His magnanimity or plenteous mercy has freely forgiven us that debt in Christ! God's mercy is rooted in His love for us. He is merciful, in large part, because He is love. Since God does love us and is merciful, He sent His Son, Jesus Christ who laid down His life and became the sacrificial lamb so that God's mercy could be extended to us. Instead of God punishing us for our sins and unrighteousness, He allowed His Son to take the condemnation in our place. That is the ultimate act of God's mercy! Rejecting or refusing this act of mercy is accepting nothingness!

Manny Pacquiao profoundly said, "Being a Christian means accepting Christ as your Saviour, your God. That's why you are called a "Christian." If you remove Christ, there's only "ian" and that means "I am nothing,"

Do you really want to accept God's ultimate act of mercy? If yes, then pray this simple prayer of salvation:

"Father God, I know that I have broken your laws and my sins have separated me from You. Please have mercy on me and forgive me all my sins. I believe that your Son, Jesus Christ died for my sins, He was resurrected from the dead and He is alive. I invite Jesus to become the Lord of my life, to rule and reign in my heart from this day forward. Please send your Holy Spirit to help me obey You, and to do Your will for the rest of my life. In Jesus' name I pray, Amen."

If you've prayed this prayer of salvation with true conviction, then you have been empowered to become a child of God and a true follower of Jesus.

This salvation work is the doing of God, and not of man! The Bible says, "But as many as received him, to them gave He power to become the sons of God, even to them that believe on His name: Which were born, not of blood, nor of the will of the flesh, nor of the will of man, but of God." (John 1:12-13)

I'm glad to welcome you to the family of God!

May I also encourage you now to find a Bible based church where you can attend regularly and concertedly with a view to growing in the knowledge of God through His Word, the Bible.

Chapter Two

WHY DO WE NEED
HIS MERCY?

Like I tried to elucidate in the introduction to this book, humanity generally is in need of His mercy because humanity is dead in iniquities and sins. It is only mercy that could have made God not to lose His temper and do away with you and I because of our sins. Love provoked Him to embrace us with an incredible mercy. The Bible says, "But God, who is rich in mercy, for his great love wherewith he loved us, Even when we were dead in sins, hath quickened us together with Christ, (by grace ye are saved;) And hath raised us up together, and made us sit together in heavenly places in Christ Jesus: That in the ages to

15

come he might shew the exceeding riches of his grace
in his kindness toward us through Christ Jesus. For by
grace are ye saved through faith; and that not of
yourselves: it is the gift of God: Not of works, lest any
man should boast." (Eph. 2:4-9)

God took our sin-dead lives and made us alive in
Christ. He did all this on His own, without any input
from us! It is vitally important to know that we need
His mercy because we are by nature children of
wrath, the Bible says, "Among whom also we all had
our conversation in times past in the lusts of our flesh,
fulfilling the desires of the flesh and of the mind; and
were by nature the children of wrath, even as others."
(Ephesians 2:3)

Mercy of God is the escape route from the wrath of
God!

We need the mercy of God because we are in the
flesh and cannot submit to or please Him on our own
ability or efforts. None of us can stand before God
and beat our chest or boast that we can please God on
our own. Our righteousness is as filthy rags in His
sight! "But we are all as an unclean thing, and all our
righteousnesses are as filthy rags; and we all do fade

as a leaf; and our iniquities, like the wind, have taken us away." (Isaiah 64:6)

Many people who depend on their strength or are obsessed with measuring their own moral muscle never get around to living it in real life.

Why do we need mercy? We need His mercy because we are unable to come to Christ or embrace Him as Lord on our own. It is the mercy or love of the Father that draws us to Christ. "No man can come to me, except the Father which hath sent me draw him: and I will raise him up at the last day." (John 6:44)

Many of us have all behaved foolishly and turned our back on God, hence the need for mercy. We have become so adroit at doing evil instead of doing good. The Bible says, "For my people is foolish, they have not known me; they are sottish children, and they have none understanding: they are wise to do evil, but to do good they have no knowledge." (Jeremiah 4:22)

We constantly need the mercy of God because as humans we are susceptible to committing sin or to doing wrong things.

Understanding Sin

Until we understand sin and the consequences of sin, we may not appreciate the magnitude of God's mercy toward us. As human beings we all have the capacity to commit sin, willingly or unwillingly. We are prone to engage in the sin of commission, that is, a sinful action or sin of omission, that is, a sinful failure to perform an action. James says: "Therefore to him that knoweth to do good, and doeth it not, to him it is sin." (James 4:17)

Sin is iniquity! Iniquity is the deviation from what is good or right, whether or not the particular act has been expressly forbidden. Iniquity has to do with our inner motivations, the very things that we so often try to keep hidden from the eyes of men and God.

Iniquities are the wrongs that spring from our own corrupt nature. Jesus said, "For from within, out of the heart of men, proceed evil thoughts, adulteries, fornications, murders, Thefts, covetousness, wickedness, deceit, lasciviousness, an evil eye, blasphemy, pride, foolishness: All these evil things come from within, and defile the man." (Mk7:21-23)

Sin is also about missing the mark; it is falling short of divine expectations. The Bible says, "For all have sinned, and come short of the glory of God;" (Rom. 3:23)

There are many areas that we have fallen short of divine expectations. For instance, in our belief system. How many of us truly believe God? Unbelief is a sin because it is an insult to the truthfulness of God. The Bible says, "He that believeth on the Son of God hath the witness in himself: he that believeth not God hath made him a liar; because he believeth not the record that God gave of his Son." (1 Jn5:10)

Someone said, "It is unbelief that shuts the door to heaven and opens it to hell. It is unbelief that rejects the Word of God and refuses Christ as saviour."

God is a holy and righteous God. He cannot tolerate sin. Sin is what separates us from Him and brings His wrath upon us. "BEHOLD, the LORD's hand is not shortened, that it cannot save; neither his ear heavy, that it cannot hear. But your iniquities have separated between you and your God, and your sins have hid his face from you, that he will not hear." (Is. 59:1-2)

Like David, many of us are vulnerable, we have weak spots which we need to work on constantly so that we will not fall into sin, especially the sin of immorality. As you well know this sin is what the enemy is using to destroy great destinies these days. David was sexually vulnerable but failed to check it and his vulnerability plunged him into the sin of adultery. These days some Christians act inappropriately toward the opposite sex. They view other people as objects to be desired.

Are you a Christian lady reading this book? Please know that it is unchristian and wrong for you to improperly display your body. You are not a prostitute! Don't be an agent of the devil to cause the downfall of a brother! You know David's fall began when he looked amorously at the body of a woman bathing. "And it came to pass in an eveningtide, that David arose from off his bed, and walked upon the roof of the king's house: and from the roof he saw a woman washing herself; and the woman was very beautiful to look upon." (2Sam 11:2)

Don't dress so seductively or carelessly, you could cause a brother to lust after you.

Are you a Christian guy reading this book? Be very vigilant. The spirit of whoredom is on the rampage!

Many of those ladies displaying or exposing their bodies are agents of the devil. Their mission is to cause your downfall. Don't become their victim! Believe me! Lust has a terrifying power. It crashes in like a strong tidal wave and sweeps all responsible thinking aside. One of my daughters in the Lord who gave in to immorality told me she forgot all the warnings and covenant of purity she entered into. It was after she finished messing up her virginity that she realised what the devil has done to her destiny via uncontrolled passion. Just five minutes of emotional madness landed her in a terrible quagmire.

Lust forces people to live for the now. Lust will not allow you to think of the future or repercussions of your immoral act. David, a man who loved God was overwhelmed as lust prevailed. No matter how much you love or serve God, if you allow lust to prevail, you may become a captive of lust, so I candidly urge you not to toy or play around with lust! By all means try to cage your strong sexual desire, so that you can enjoy a robust relationship with God.

Just recently after a ministration in one church, a young lady walked up to me for counseling and said, "I'm an addict! I'm addicted to porn!" To this lady, porn has become so stubborn that it has gotten a life of its own. It has become a lord over her life. Porn addiction is a terrible sinful habit that is ravaging both

21

guys and ladies today. No doubt, many people today are struggling with pornography! The challenge is that not many of them have realized or recognized what a terrible toll this habit is taking on them and their relationship with the Lord. Many don't even see anything wrong with it! My beloved, I must be blunt with you here! You may not commit physical adultery or fornication but you are not exonerated! In the light of Jesus standard, if mere looking with a view to lusting after a woman could categorize you with adulterers, then porn is a grievous sin of adultery! "But I say unto you, That whosoever looketh on a woman to lust after her hath committed adultery with her already in his heart." (Mat. 5:28)

God saw David's sin and hated it. But the way David responded to his sin impressed God. David did not justify himself or give excuses for his sin as many of us would do today. David was totally broken. Ps 51 reveals how deeply he understood the horror of his sin. It was very painful for him to realise that he had offended his Holy God. These days how many Christians would feel bad for hurting a loving Father? Many would readily justify their sins by saying or putting up an attitude that: "Everyone is doing it, I'm not an exception." Or "God understands and He will always be merciful."

A true child of God cannot respond with a carefree attitude.

Mercy is a powerful tool for the transformation or regeneration of a sinner. It is by God's mercy and grace that you can be transformed from a sinner to a saint, from a nobody to somebody; from an ordinary person to an extraordinary person!

How can we escape the wrath of God? Mercy!

How can we be free from bondage of sin? Mercy!

How can we get back to God? Mercy!

The way back to God is not humanity determined. It is God determined.

So many people stop at the level of confession, without moving on to the level of forsaking their sin. You cannot only confess your way back to God and think that you have satisfied or fulfilled His requirement for mercy. For you to experience mercy, you must confess and forsake your sin. The Bible says, "He that covereth his sins shall not prosper: but whoso confesseth and forsaketh them shall have mercy." (Pro.28:13)

03

Chapter Three

CRYING OUT FOR MERCY

Is it scriptural to cry out for His mercy? Yes! People who procured His mercy at one time or the other in the Bible did cry out for it. "And he cried, saying, Jesus, thou Son of David, have mercy on me. And they which went before rebuked him, that he should hold his peace: but he cried so much the more, Thou Son of David, have mercy on me. And Jesus stood, and commanded him to be brought unto him: and when he was come near, he asked him, Saying, What wilt thou that I shall do unto thee? And he said, Lord, that I may receive my sight. And Jesus said unto him, Receive thy sight: thy faith hath saved thee. And immediately he received his sight, and followed him, glorifying God: and all the people, when they saw it, gave praise unto God." (Lk. 18:38-43)

The merciful God, as typified by Jesus, will not turn anyone down who genuinely cries out in desperation for mercy. The blind man's cry or heartfelt prayer drew the attention of Jesus and positioned him for healing. Are you in need of mercy in any area of your life? Then begin to engage the power of prayers. Cry out for mercy unashamedly and boldly; go forth and approach the throne of grace, ask God to have mercy on you. The Bible says, "Let us therefore come boldly unto the throne of grace, that we may obtain mercy, and find grace to help in time of need." (Heb. 4:16)

12 most auspicious times to cry out for His Mercy:

1. At a Time of Weakness

"Have mercy upon me, O LORD; for I am weak: O LORD, heal me; for my bones are vexed."

(Ps. 6:2)

You are meant to cry out for mercy when you sense any form of weakness in your life. Are you physically, spiritually, mentally, emotionally or financially weak

26

or challenged? Then you are in your most auspicious season to cry out for mercy. Cry out for mercy when you are at your lowest ebb. Some Christians have great weakness for alcohol and sex. They cannot just stop drinking or lusting after any lady in skirt. Cry out for mercy so that the Lord may help you from falling into sin or living in sin. Cry out for mercy when all hope seems lost or you are despondent.

2. At a Time of Trouble

"Have mercy upon me, O LORD, for I am in trouble: mine eye is consumed with grief, yea, my soul and my belly." (Ps. 31:9)

Are you in trouble of any kind, shape or size?

Are you in the midst of a mighty ocean of difficulties? Are you passing through hell right now? Then cry out like David, "Have mercy upon me, O LORD; consider my trouble which I suffer of them that hate me, thou that liftest me up from the gates of death:" (Ps. 9:13)

3. At a Time of Desolation and Affliction

"Turn thee unto me, and have mercy upon me; for I am desolate and afflicted." (Ps. 25:16)

27

Are you desolate and afflicted? You need His mercy!

Are you deserted by people? You need His mercy!

Are you in a state of bleak and dismal emptiness? You need His mercy! Maybe your life has been stressed up, you are unhappy or lonely. My surest antidote for you is that you must turn to God and cry out for His mercy; and He will surely satisfy you with His victories and deliverances.

4. At a Time of Indebtedness

"Then the Lord of that servant was moved with compassion, and loosed him, and forgave him the debt." (Mat. 18:27)

Are you a chronic debtor reading this book? There is hope for you! I see forgiveness coming your way right now. I prophesy to you that God of all mercies will cause your creditor to write off your debt in Jesus name.

There is no glory or honour in being a debtor. The agony or humiliation of indebtedness can be very excruciating. If you have ever owed someone or a bank some money, you will understand! I know some people who have been harassed and bombarded with threats for their indebtedness. I am of firm conviction that God does not want us to be indebted. The only debt He wants us to owe is that of love. What we owe people is love as children of God. For the Bible says, "Owe no man any thing, but to love one another: for he that loveth another hath fulfilled the law." (Rom. 13:8)

5. *At a Time when you need Forgiveness*

"Have mercy upon me, O God, according to thy lovingkindness: according unto the multitude of thy tender mercies blot out my transgressions." (Ps. 51:1)

Have you sinned, transgressed or offended God or someone lately? You sure need forgiveness! God is a good God and He is ever ready to forgive you if only you cry out for His plenteous mercy! The Bible says, "By mercy and truth iniquity is purged: and by the fear of the LORD men depart from evil." (Pro. 16:6)

Please do not cover your sins, do not justify or give excuses. If you do, you will not prosper. "He that covereth his sins shall not prosper: but whoso confesseth and forsaketh them shall have mercy." (Pro. 28:13)

The wicked has hope in God if only he forsakes his evil ways, his unrighteous imaginations and return unto the Lord in genuine repentance. "Let the wicked forsake his way, and the unrighteous man his thoughts: and let him return unto the LORD, and he will have mercy upon him; and to our God, for he will abundantly pardon."

(Is. 55:7)

You can serve as an advocate like Moses! I mean you can stand in the gap for others by pleading for them so that God may pardon their sins. "Pardon, I beseech thee, the iniquity of this people according unto the greatness of thy mercy, and as thou hast forgiven this people, from Egypt even until now." (Num. 14:19)

Forgiveness can cheaply be secured when you confess your sins or iniquities to God!

"If we confess our sins, he is faithful and just to forgive us our sins, and to cleanse us from all unrighteousness. If we say that we have not sinned, we make him a liar, and his word is not in us." (1John 1:9-10)

6. At a Time when you need Strength

"O turn unto me, and have mercy upon me; give thy strength unto thy servant, and save the son of thine handmaid." (Ps. 86:16)

You need to be strong in order to face the challenges of life. You need physical, spiritual, emotional and mental stamina necessary in dealing with situations or events that are distressing and difficult. The truth is that it takes strength to overcome the plethora of issues bothering humanity today. To gain motion in life, strength is required. When your energy or strength is abated or being sapped, cry out for His mercy, and He will exchange His strength with your weakness. "And he said unto me, My grace is sufficient for thee: for my strength is made perfect in weakness. Most gladly therefore will I rather glory in my infirmities, that the power of Christ may rest upon me."

(2 Cor. 12:9)

7. At a Time when you need Favour

"Thou shalt arise, and have mercy upon Zion: for the time to favour her, yea, the set time, is come." (Ps. 102:13)

Do you want an overflowing and overgenerous preferential treatment? Favour is it! Do you want an act of kindness beyond what is due or usual? If yes, then you need favour! And for you to be favoured you need His mercy. In life, you sure need favour at one point or the other. One day of favour is superior to a thousand days of labour! Your time to be favoured is here, but you need His mercy to procure His favour. My prayer is that God may satisfy you early with His mercy so that you will rejoice always over His favour at work in your life. "O satisfy us early with thy mercy; that we may rejoice and be glad all our days." (Ps. 90:14)

(For more light on the subject of favour, please read my book, "How to obtain favour from God and man")

8. *At a Time when you need Direction*

"Thou in thy mercy hast led forth the people which thou hast redeemed: thou hast guided them in thy strength unto thy holy habitation. (Ex. 15:13)

It was on the premise of His mercy that God led His people out of Egypt. God is set to lead and direct you to your destination in life. There is nothing as wonderful as knowing where you are heading in life.

Many people are stranded in the journey of life because they lack direction. An auspicious time to plead for mercy of God is when you are at a crossroad, not knowing where to head. God by His mercy shall direct and lead you aright. "They shall not hunger nor thirst; neither shall the heat nor sun smite them: for he that hath mercy on them shall lead them, even by the springs of water shall he guide them."

(Is. 49:10)

9. At a Time when you need Restoration

"And I will shew mercies unto you, that he may have mercy upon you, and cause you to return to your own land." (Jer. 42:12)

Do you need restoration in any area of your life?

Have you been demoted from your position and you want a reinstatement or restoration? "And he restored the chief butler unto his butlership again; and he gave the cup into Pharaoh's hand:" (Gen. 40:21)

Has your relationship with God packed up and you desperately need a miracle of reconciliation? If yes, then it's time to plead or cry out for the mercy of God.

Plead that the Lord by His mercy may restore unto you the joy of His salvation!

"Restore unto me the joy of thy salvation; and uphold me with thy free spirit." (Ps. 51:12)

10. *At a Time when you need Healing*

"For indeed he was sick nigh unto death: but God had mercy on him; and not on him only, but on me also, lest I should have sorrow upon sorrow." (Phil 2:27)

God's mercy is designed for your Healing! Are you sick in your body? It will require the mercy of God to get you off the sick bed. Epaphroditus, Apostle Paul's able companion in ministry was sick to the point of death but God's mercy rescued him from the jaws of sickness and death. From the earthly Ministry of Jesus Christ, we can deduce that God designed His mercy for the healing of man. After cleansing and healing the demonic man, He told him to return home and declare the mercy that God has shown to him. "Howbeit Jesus suffered him not, but saith unto him, Go home to thy friends, and tell them how great things the Lord hath done for thee, and hath had compassion on thee. And he departed, and began to publish in Decapolis how great things Jesus had done for him: and all men did marvel." (Mk. 5:19-20)

11. At a Time when you need Answers from God

"Hear, O LORD, when I cry with my voice: have mercy also upon me, and answer me." (Ps. 27:7)

I have realised that it will require the mercy of God to procure answers from God. It is His mercy upon you that makes Him to answer you speedily. Having an assurance of response from God when you call upon Him can be heartwarming and enthralling. Cry out for God's mercy to command instant or speedy answers always from God.

12. At a Time when you need Mercy from man

"And hath extended mercy unto me before the king, and his counsellors, and before all the king's mighty princes. And I was strengthened as the hand of the LORD my God was upon me, and I gathered together out of Israel chief men to go up with me." (Ezra 7:28)

Does man possess the power or capacity to show mercy? Yes! Is it scriptural for you to cry out or pray to find mercy in the sight of mere mortal? Yes! Can God extend His mercy unto you in the sight of man? Yes! Mercy is received and enjoyed on the basis of divine approval or permission! The Bible says, "... A man can receive nothing, except it be given him from heaven." (John 3:27)

If you need mercy from man, the winning key is that you must first secure it from God, if not you will be disappointed. Man is a mere tool in the invisible hands of God. Except the Lord grants you mercy in the sight of man, your quest to procuring mercy will be a far cry! The Bible says, "O Lord, I beseech thee, let now thine ear be attentive to the prayer of thy servant, and to the prayer of thy servants, who desire to fear thy name: and prosper, I pray thee, thy servant this day, and grant him mercy in the sight of this man. For I was the king's cupbearer."

(Neh. 1:11)

Chapter four

7 CHARACTERISTICS OF GOD'S MERCY

1. God's mercy is everlasting

"For the LORD is good; his mercy is everlasting; and his truth endureth to all generations."

(Ps. 100:5)

God's mercy is long lasting! It is enduring, existing and continuing without end. His mercy is immortal and eternal. It is not a temporary phenomenon! It is not to be enjoyed today, and tomorrow is no longer available to be enjoyed. His mercy can be secured, activated and enjoyed everyday, every time and everywhere. Mercy is a divine attribute as such it is designed to be everlasting like the Everlasting God. God gives His people everlasting possessions. For instance, the Bible says, "And I will give unto thee, and to thy seed after thee, the land wherein thou art a stranger, all the land of Canaan, for an everlasting possession; and I will be their God." (Gen. 17:8)

We all are witnesses to the calculated attempt by enemies of Israel to uproot her from the land of Canaan for several years now, but to no avail. These Arab enemies of Israel could not, and will not achieve their nefarious agenda or dreams simply because of the everlasting dimension of God's promise. I was privileged to visit Israel a couple of years ago and I can attest to the faithfulness of God to His promises to Israel. God has really blessed this tiny nation with so much capacity to command fruitfulness in all areas of human endeavour.

2. God's mercy is plenteous

God's mercy is not just everlasting but also plenteous and abundant. "The LORD is merciful and gracious, slow to anger, and plenteous in mercy." (Ps. 103:8)

"Blessed be the God and Father of our Lord Jesus Christ, which according to his abundant mercy hath begotten us again unto a lively hope by the resurrection of Jesus Christ from the dead," (1 Pt. 1:3)

In the two verses above, we are reminded of the extravagance of God's mercy, and the expansiveness of the blessings God confers on us on the basis of His mercy. We can take advantage of His mega mercy by placing a demand for mercy at all times. There is no shortage or short supply of His mercy! As a born again child of God, you are entitled to abundant life in Christ Jesus! "The thief cometh not, but for to steal, and to kill, and to destroy: I am come that they might have life, and that they might have it more abundantly." (John 10:10)

3. God's mercy is great

"For as the heaven is high above the earth, so great is his mercy toward them that fear him." (Ps. 103:11)

Do you fear God? If yes, then you are a candidate of His great mercy! You can enjoy great mercy from Him. In His great mercy, there is a compelling invitation like this: "My beloved child, whatever you have done wrong, no matter the magnitude of your sins, no matter how far you have been away from Me, it doesn't matter, you are still welcome back home." It is God's great mercy that makes your coming back home easy, and also makes your falling into God's hands a better and superior option.

"And David said unto Gad, I am in a great strait: let us fall now into the hand of the LORD; for his mercies are great: and let me not fall into the hand of man." (2 Sam. 24:14)

4. God's mercy is good

"But do thou for me, O GOD the Lord, for thy name's sake: because thy mercy is good, deliver thou me." (Ps. 109:21)

There is nothing evil about God's mercy! Mercy is good! Have you enjoyed the rich and good mercy of God? If yes, then you are not permitted to just live as you please, or please yourself. Having received God's good mercy you are meant to manifest mercy by being rich in mercy and doing abundant good works. Mercy is the energiser of good works. His mercy energises you to be merciful, to do good works, and to abound in good works.

Have you realised this truth? It is His good mercy that saved you, and not by good works. But now that you are saved or forgiven by His mercy, you are saved to save others. You are forgiven to forgive others. Your life must emit mercy at all times.

5. God's mercy is manifold

God's mercy is manifold. It has many different forms or elements. Like diamond, it has innumerable facets. Every vantage point reflects a new insight into the gracious resources of our Lord. It is both humbling and faith-building to be reminded of the majestic diversity of God's mercy. The Bible says, "Therefore thou deliveredst them into the hand of their enemies, who vexed them: and in the time of their trouble, when they cried unto thee, thou heardest them from heaven; and according to thy manifold mercies thou gavest them saviours, who saved them out of the hand of their enemies."

(Neh. 9:27)

God's mercy moves Him to send you destiny helpers or saviours when you cry out for His intervention. And these helpers will help deliver you from all your enemies. His mercy will never allow you to be destroyed or abandoned. Help is coming your way on the platform of mercy right now! His mercy will usher in a fresh tenderness and visitation. And when He visits, your life will never remain the same!

"Through the tender mercy of our God; whereby the dayspring from on high hath visited us," (Lk 1:78)

6. God's mercy follows us

"Surely goodness and mercy shall follow me all the days of my life: and I will dwell in the house of the LORD for ever." (Ps. 23:6)

What a wonderful assurance that wherever we find ourselves or wherever we go, His mercy follows us. That means we don't have to be in a particular place to enjoy His mercy. Everywhere is ok or apt to enjoy His mercy. Beloved, His mercy is pursuing you right now! You shall be satisfied with His mercy early enough to accomplish your goals, dreams and visions. You will have every reason to rejoice and be glad indeed. "O satisfy us early with thy mercy; that we may rejoice and be glad all our days."

(Ps. 90:14)

7. God's mercy can be taken away

"I will be his father, and he shall be my son: and I will not take my mercy away from him, as I took it from him that was before thee:" (1 Chro. 17:13)

May I conclude this chapter with a warning: Don't take His mercy for granted. Because from the above scripture we can see clearly that mercy can be taken away from one! I do believe that mercy can be taken away when one takes His mercy for granted. How do we take His mercy for granted? You may ask. By living continually in sin, and not repenting or forsaking of one's sins. The Bible says, "What shall we say then? Shall we continue in sin, that grace may abound? God forbid. How shall we, that are dead to sin, live any longer therein?" (Rom. 6:1-2)

"What then? shall we sin, because we are not under the law, but under grace? God forbid. Know ye not, that to whom ye yield yourselves servants to obey, his servants ye are to whom ye obey; whether of sin unto death, or of obedience unto righteousness?" (Rom. 6:15-16)

You take God's mercy for granted if you only appreciate His mercy and forgiveness, but refuse to jettison or rid yourself of sin or unrighteousness. I

43

have seen or heard of brethren perpetrating a wholesome lifestyle of sin by claiming or relying on these verses of scripture: "For he knoweth our frame; he remembereth that we are dust" (Ps. 103:14)

"For a just man falleth seven times, and riseth up again: but the wicked shall fall into mischief." (Pro 24:16)

"Then came Peter to him, and said, Lord, how oft shall my brother sin against me, and I forgive him? till seven times? Jesus saith unto him, I say not unto thee, Until seven times: but, Until seventy times seven." (Mat 18:21-22)

Truly, His forgiveness is great and repetitive! But it should not be a justification to live in sin as a lifestyle. As a Christian you may stumble into sin occasionally but you are not expected to live in it.

A pig likes or treasures muddy water, because that's the pig's natural habitat. You are not a pig. You are a sheep. If you find yourself in sin, get out by all means by crying out for His mercy.

His mercy is exceptionally great and good, but don't ever try to use it as an excuse not to work on your sin problems and seek to overcome them.

To remain in sin perpetually is to take His mercy for granted. I cannot overemphasise this point enough! There is a limit to God's mercy or forgiveness. Esau discovered this limit when, "he sought it with tears." but it was too late for him. (Heb. 12:17) True and authentic repentance will produce a positive reaction from God in every circumstance. Let Him see your sincere desire and effort to overcome every besetting sin.

05

Chapter 5

SHOWING MERCY
TO PEOPLE

As a profound beneficiary of God's goodness and love, which He ably demonstrated by forgiving you all your sins and transgressions, it is incumbent on you or it behooves you to demonstrate to others what you have received from God. Have you enjoyed mercy from God? Let others also enjoy mercy from you. Have you enjoyed forgiveness? Let other people enjoy forgiveness from you! You can provoke forgiveness from God the Father if you forgive people who have hurt or wronged you. The Bible says, "For if ye forgive men their trespasses, your heavenly Father will also forgive you: But if ye forgive not men

47

their trespasses, neither will your Father forgive your trespasses."

(Mat. 6:14-15)

If God showed you His compassion by forgiving all your sins, you too must extend this good gesture to others who are indebted to you. Don't be like this wicked servant who enjoyed forgiveness but was unwilling to show same to his fellow servant. Please read this passage: "The servant therefore fell down, and worshipped him, saying, Lord, have patience with me, and I will pay thee all. Then the lord of that servant was moved with compassion, and loosed him, and forgave him the debt. But the same servant went out, and found one of his fellowservants, which owed him an hundred pence: and he laid hands on him, and took him by the throat, saying, Pay me that thou owest. And his fellowservant fell down at his feet, and besought him, saying, Have patience with me, and I will pay thee all. And he would not: but went and cast him into prison, till he should pay the debt. So when his fellowservants saw what was done, they were very sorry, and came and told unto their lord all that was done. Then his lord, after that he had called him, said unto him, O thou wicked servant, I forgave thee all that debt, because thou desiredst me: Shouldest not thou also have had compassion on thy fellowservant, even as I had pity on thee? And his lord was wroth, and delivered him to the tormentors, till he should pay all that was due unto him. So likewise shall my heavenly Father do also unto you, if ye from your hearts forgive not every one his brother their trespasses." (Mat.18:26-35)

The Bible says, "Be ye therefore followers of God, as dear children" (Eph. 5:1)

One veritable way to authenticate or validate your true sonship is by showing forth the nature of God. You cannot claim to be a child of God or a true follower of God if you are not willing and prepared to show mercy to people who hurt or wrong you. As a child of God you possess the intrinsic nature of God to show mercy. You are naturally endowed and empowered to show mercy.

As your Heavenly Father is rich in mercy you too must be rich in works of mercy. You must be merciful in giving and forgiving. "Be ye therefore merciful, as your Father also is merciful."

(Luke 6:36)

It is an aberration for a wicked person to show mercy. Why? Because he does not have the capacity to do so. Like I always say, the devil cannot show mercy. It is not in his nature. Satan does not have the capacity to be merciful. His agents or cohorts can never give true love or show mercy.

Being merciful is about your capacity to be kind and good natured or your capacity to forgive someone who is vulnerable and has done something heinous. Mercy overrides or sets aside questions of equity, justice, vengeance, or even blame. Mercy does not ask about what someone deserves, but about what the person needs. A criminal deserves punishment, but he or she needs mercy. Mercy triumphs over judgement.

Without mercy, the world would be a harsh place to live in. I don't know about other folks, but I know this about myself that when I cogitate or recognize the gift of mercy that I have received graciously from God, I deliberately and concertedly condition my mind to always show others the same gift. If you are callous and wicked to others the same seed you have sown awaits you! If you refused to show mercy when someone wronged you, the same seed you have sown awaits you. If you have not been merciful to others, don't ever expect someone else to be merciful to you. It is what you sow you shall reap.

I love sharing the story of Adonibezek, a wicked King who never had mercy in his heart for his captives. He equally reaped what he sowed in the lives of those he captured.

"And Judah went up; and the LORD delivered the Canaanites and the Perizzites into their hand: and they slew of them in Bezek ten thousand men. And they found Adonibezek in Bezek: and they fought against him, and they slew the Canaanites and the Perizzites. But Adonibezek fled; and they pursued after him, and caught him, and cut off his thumbs and his great toes. And Adonibezek said, Threescore and ten kings, having their thumbs and their great toes cut off, gathered their meat under my table: as I have done, so God hath requited me. And they brought him to Jerusalem, and there he died." (Judges 1:4-7)

You are a vessel of mercy! May this truth be fully entrenched into you.

"And that he might make known the riches of his glory on the vessels of mercy, which he had afore prepared unto glory," (Rom. 9:23)

Every born again Christian is a vessel of mercy, and not a vessel of wrath. God said to Moses, "I will have mercy on whom I will have mercy, and I will have compassion on whom I will have compassion. So then it is not of him that willeth, nor of him that runneth, but of God that sheweth mercy." (Rom. 9:15-16)

As God's dear and pleasant child, you have enjoyed His unspeakable mercy like Ephraim, therefore you must be prepared to show mercy to others. "Is Ephraim my dear son? is he a pleasant child? for since I spake against him, I do earnestly remember him still: therefore my bowels are troubled for him; I will surely have mercy upon him, saith the LORD." (Jer. 31:20)

Only the vessel of His mercy can show mercy! Therefore it is a taboo not to show mercy if you are truly a bonafide child of God. It is absolutely wrong not to show mercy when it is within your power or capacity to do so.

May I conclude this chapter by urging you to have it as a topmost priority in your heart to show mercy to others, for the Bible says, "Thus speaketh the LORD of hosts, saying, Execute true judgment, and shew

mercy and compassions every man to his brother:"
(Zechariah 7:9)

Chapter 6

7 QUALITIES THAT PROCURE MERCY

The Bible says, "And the spies saw a man come forth out of the city, and they said unto him, Shew us, we pray thee, the entrance into the city, and we will shew thee mercy." (Judges 1:24)

From the above passage it is apt to assert that one can procure mercy. There is what to do to engender mercy. There is what to be to command mercy!

It feels good to enjoy mercy! It feels good to be forgiven. It feels good to be shown compassion!

But are there rare qualities one must imbibe or cultivate in order to procure mercy? Yes! Certainly!

My duty in this chapter is to help you identify seven qualities, and to also show you how to take advantage of them for your optimum benefit.

I am of firm conviction that you want to procure mercy, as such modeling the following qualities is highly critical. The more of these qualities you command the higher your chances of becoming all that God has packaged for you via His mercy!

1. Quality of Love

"And shewing mercy unto thousands of them that love me, and keep my commandments." (Ex. 20:6)

Do you truly love God? Is God the love of your life? Do you have an intense feeling of deep affection for God? Do you have a great interest and pleasure in God? If yes, then you are a candidate to procure the mercy of God! Those that find much pleasure in God are candidates of His mercy. Also those that extend God's love to others via acts of good works or charity are bonafide candidates of God's mercy.

2. Quality of Mercy Seed

"Be not deceived; God is not mocked: for whatsoever a man soweth, that shall he also reap." (Gal. 6:7)

If you are a planter of mercy seed in the lives of people around you, you automatically qualify for mercy harvest. No mercy seed! No mercy harvest! Period! The Bible says, "With the merciful thou wilt shew thyself merciful, and with the upright man thou wilt shew thyself upright." (2 Sam. 22:26)

Jesus said, "Blessed are the merciful: for they shall obtain mercy." (Mat. 5:7)

3. Quality of Fear of God

"And his mercy is on them that fear him from generation to generation." (Luke 1:50)

Fear of God is not about being afraid of God. But about showing reverence or deep respect to God. It is about regarding the person of God above all things and all people, no matter how they are highly placed in the society. These days some Christians regard the person of their leaders more than God. What a shame! For instance, they cannot make or take phone calls in the presence of their superiors, but they can do that in the presence of God. Have you not seen some making calls, sending SMS, and even browsing the Internet while fellowship or church service is ongoing? Indulging in these disrespectful acts only show that you do not have regard for God. Period! Please honour His presence except you don't believe He is in your midst. If your gathering is in His name, then expect Him to be present! The Bible says, "For where two or three are gathered together in my name, there am I in the midst of them."

(Mat. 18:20)

God shows mercy to those that honour and hold Him in high esteem.

4. Quality of Divine presence

"But the LORD was with Joseph, and shewed him mercy, and gave him favour in the sight of the keeper of the prison." (Gen. 39:21)

Joseph was shown mercy because God tabernacled with him. The God in him provided all he needed at any given time. If he needed favour in the sight of Potiphar or the keeper of the prison, the God that dwelt with him was capable of remote controlling or orchestrating that into his life. There is a beauty far more excellent than physical beauty, and that is the beauty of the presence of God in a man's life. If God is with any man, several blessings result. If God be for you who can be against you! Nobody! God's manifest presence is the key to your undeniable mercy harvests. It is impossible to procure mercy without divine presence. You cannot wish Divine presence into place or reality but you can provoke it into existence by making your life conducive for God to dwell in.

5. *Quality of Uprightness*

"And Solomon said, Thou hast shewed unto thy servant David my father great mercy, according as he walked before thee in truth, and in righteousness, and in uprightness of heart with thee; and thou hast kept for him this great kindness, that thou hast given him a son to sit on his throne, as it is this day." (1 Kings 3:6)

God is the God of all generations! The God of David is still our God today. He showed David great mercy because David walked before Him in truth, righteousness and uprightness of heart. If we cultivate the same quality of uprightness or righteousness He will show us His great mercy. Sin is what separates man from God, but glory be to Him for the gift of His Son Jesus Christ who paid the ultimate price for our sins. He became sin for us and His blood was shed to wash us clean of all our iniquities.

We need to continue to pursue or press toward living a life of righteousness or uprightness. God is ever faithful to release mercy to His servants that walk before Him with their whole heart and those that keep His covenant and testimonies. The Bible says, "And he said, LORD God of Israel, there is no God like thee, in heaven above, or on earth beneath, who keepest covenant and mercy with thy servants that walk before thee with all their heart:" (1 Kings 8:23)

"All the paths of the LORD are mercy and truth unto such as keep his covenant and his testimonies." (Ps. 25:10)

6. Quality of Goodness

"Do they not err that devise evil? but mercy and truth shall be to them that devise good." (Pro. 14:22). People who are good and always devise good stand a great chance of procuring mercy than those that are evil and devise evil. The Bible says, "Do good, O LORD, unto those that be good, and to them that are upright in their hearts." (Ps. 125:4)

It pays to get accustomed to doing good than doing evil. People that are accustomed to doing evil always find it difficult to do good. "Can the Ethiopian change his skin, or the leopard his spots? then may ye also do good, that are accustomed to do evil." (Jer. 13:23)

As humans none of us can do good except we are empowered by the good Lord. We can devise and do good because the God of all goodness lives within us, as He has empowered us to love and do good even to our enemies. Great rewards await people who are good and do good to others. "But love ye your enemies, and do good, and lend, hoping for nothing again; and your reward shall be great, and ye shall be the children of the Highest: for he is kind unto the unthankful and to the evil." (Lk. 6:35)

7. Quality of Service

"Behold now, thy servant hath found grace in thy sight, and thou hast magnified thy mercy, which thou hast shewed unto me in saving my life; and I cannot escape to the mountain, lest some evil take me, and I die:" (Gen. 19:19)

Service to God can procure His mercy! Only His servants qualify for mercy. One of the most important things you can do to command mercy is to keep serving the Lord and His kingdom. The Bible says, "But seek ye first the kingdom of God, and his righteousness; and all these things shall be added unto you." (Mat. 6:33)

Mercy is part of the additions promised in the above passage.

You don't have to be an ordained clergy to see yourself as a servant of God. Every born again Christian can serve God in one capacity or the other. We are all endowed and empowered to minister to God and one another. The Bible says, "As every man hath received the gift, even so minister the same one to another, as good stewards of the manifold grace of God. If any man speak, let him speak as the oracles of God; if any man minister, let him do it as of the ability which God giveth: that God in all things may be glorified through Jesus Christ, to whom be praise and dominion for ever and ever. Amen." (1Peter4:10-11)

Resolve today to get engaged in kingdom service! What is Kingdom Service? You may ask. Kingdom service is all about serving God's people in the church and serving God's purpose in the world. Kingdom service is also about expanding the kingdom of God via deliberate and concerted soul winning efforts. It's not the will of God that any soul should perish in hell fire!

As God's servant you are a candidate to procure and enjoy God's mercy!

Chapter 7

DEVELOPING A HEART OF COMPASSION

"But a certain Samaritan, as he journeyed, came where he was: and when he saw him, he had compassion on him, And went to him, and bound up his wounds, pouring in oil and wine, and set him on his own beast, and brought him to an inn, and took care of him. And on the morrow when he departed, he took out two pence, and gave them to the host, and said unto him, Take care of him; and whatsoever thou spendest more, when I come again, I will repay thee. Which now of these three, thinkest thou, was neighbour unto him that fell among the thieves?

And he said, He that shewed mercy on him. Then said Jesus unto him, Go, and do thou likewise." (Lk. 10:33-37)

Jesus said in the above passage, "Go and do thou likewise." This command or instruction from the Lord lends credence to the fact that each one of us can develop a heart of compassion. His instruction also buttresses the fact that we all have the potential or what it takes to show compassion to people in need.

What is Compassion?

A wiseman said, "Compassion is about investing whatever is necessary to heal the hurts of others."

Compassion is one's ability to respond mercifully to the suffering of others. It is a powerful force that motivates people to go out of their way to help others who are hurting spiritually, physically, mentally, materially, financially and emotionally. For instance, the Good Samaritan in the above scripture went out of his way to empathise or consider the hurts or pains of the battered man with a view to ameliorating his suffering. He arose with active, strong, compelling desire to alleviate the man's suffering by all means not minding the risk or danger involved.

The proverbial saying that "People do not care how much you know, until they know how much you care." absolutely commands a measure of truth. The truth is that compassion is superior to knowledge. Except you go out of your comfort zone to show compassion, nobody cares about your robust knowledge of someone suffering or in need. Except you add action to your knowledge, compassion is not in place.

Majority of us are a bunch of sympathisers, not empathisers. Empathy is superior to sympathy. When you empathise you understand and share the feelings of the person concerned. You like to do something practically to alleviate the person's suffering or meet the person's need. Sympathy driven persons are passive, only showing pity at the condition of the person without necessarily doing anything. While empathy driven persons on the other hand are active contributors to the challenge at hand. The Bible says, "Remember them that are in bonds, as bound with them; and them which suffer adversity, as being yourselves also in the body." (Heb 13:3)

Do you know people who are hurting or vulnerable and need urgent care and protection? It is what you do about your knowledge that matters. And it is compassion that can propel you to take action with a view to solving the problems which you are aware of.

Jesus Christ is our perfect example or template of compassion! During His earthly ministry, He was always "moved with compassion" to attend to the needs of people. "Then Jesus called his disciples unto him, and said, I have compassion on the multitude, because they continue with me now three days, and have nothing to eat: and I will not send them away fasting, lest they faint in the way." (Mat. 15:32)

Jesus knew that this people had been with Him for three days without food. He was moved to act because He would not want them to faint on their way home. This is compassion! This is empathy! His disciples on the other hand knew about the people's condition but couldn't do anything.

Compassion can move you to do the unthinkable!

For instance, it was the spirit of compassion that motivated or moved Jesus to touch and heal a leper. "And there came a leper to him, beseeching him, and kneeling down to him, and saying unto him, If thou wilt, thou canst make me clean. And Jesus, moved with compassion, put forth his hand, and touched him, and saith unto him, I will; be thou clean. And as

68

soon as he had spoken, immediately the leprosy departed from him, and he was cleansed." (Mark 1:40-42)

Jesus' compassion was not restricted to the area of healing alone. He demonstrated compassion when He heard that John the Baptist was murdered. Jesus took His disciples apart into a remote area near Bethsaida. But the multitudes followed after Him. The Bible says that Jesus "had compassion on them, because they were as sheep not having a shepherd"

Just think about this! The Lord set aside His own grief for His murdered cousin, a righteous man of God, to minister to these people who so desperately needed direction in their lives. What a man of compassion! How many of us can put aside our personal needs and challenges just to meet the needs and challenges of others?

We can feel the pain of others if we are selfless.

Jesus cared for the afflicted because He was selfless. I'm of firm conviction that Jesus is still in the business of caring for people that are hurting today. But He can only carry out this divine business through you and I. When our compassion loses its sharpness we can no longer become His true ambassadors.

We all want a better world, but our desire to have a better world will be a far cry if we refuse to adorn ourselves with the garment of selflessness and compassion. May the Lord clothe us today with His garment of compassion!

Why do we need to develop compassion?

We need to develop compassion because of the reward benefit attached. We reap whatever we sow. The Bible says, "Be not deceived; God is not mocked: for whatsoever a man soweth, that shall he also reap." (Gal. 6:7)

If we sow quality compassion seed in the lives of people around us, we automatically qualify for compassion harvest. If we are empathic toward others, God will move people to be empathic toward us as well. If we are concerned about others, people will show concern toward us. The Bible says, "With the merciful thou wilt shew thyself merciful, and with the upright man thou wilt shew thyself upright." (2 Sam. 22:26)

70

Jesus said, "Blessed are the merciful: for they shall obtain mercy." (Mat. 5:7)

Like mercy, compassion begets compassion.

We need to develop or cultivate compassion because we have been instructed to show compassion to one another. As born again Christians, we are enjoined to be compassionate toward one another. The Bible says, "Finally, be ye all of one mind, having compassion one of another, love as brethren, be pitiful, be courteous:" (1 Peter 3:8)

We need to develop compassion because like mercy, it is an instrument for subduing our iniquities and casting our sins into the depths of the sea. It is compassion that helps or empowers us to forgive people who hurt us. "He will turn again, he will have compassion upon us; he will subdue our iniquities; and thou wilt cast all their sins into the depths of the sea." (Micah 7:19)

We need to cultivate or develop compassion because it is the quality we must have, to touch lives positively. We need compassion to bear the burden of others. The Bible says, "Bear ye one another's burdens, and so fulfill the law of Christ." (Gal. 6:2)

We are obligated to add value to others especially those in crisis or desperate conditions.

We need to develop compassion because of the joy or happiness we derive touching lives and making others happy. You can't selflessly care for people and not be happy! That is the superior goal of showing compassion. Compassionate people find their great fulfillment or sense of significance by making others happier. If we agree that it is a common aim of each of us to strive to be happy, then compassion is one of the main tools for achieving that happiness. It is therefore of utmost importance that we cultivate compassion in our lives and practice compassion regularly.

We need to develop compassion because it is a promoter and preserver of destiny. You may not know whose destiny you're preserving by developing the heart of compassion and engaging in compassionate efforts. You might be preserving a Moses of your generation! Just imagine for a second little Moses not enjoying compassion. The Bible says, "And when she had opened it, she saw the child: and, behold, the babe wept. And she had compassion on

him, and said, This is one of the Hebrews' children."
(Exodus 2:6)

Without compassion as displayed by Pharaoh's
daughter, Moses would not have lived to fulfill
destiny. He would have been killed like other Hebrew
male babies, after all, there was a subsisting law that
all male children be killed.

Compassion is a preserver of life and destiny.

We need to develop compassion because Jesus Christ
showed us a worthy example of compassion. As
disciples of Christ, we are meant to follow in His
footsteps. We are to feel the pains of others like He
did during His earthly ministry. Someone said, "You
can never heal the needs you do not feel. Tearless
hearts can never be heralds of compassion." The
easiest way to make a hurting world happy is to
practice compassion. Compassion is the quality we
must put on in order to bring harmony and happiness
to our families, communities and our world generally.
A world without compassion is an endangered world.
I believe compassion to be one of the few things we
can practice that will bring immediate and long-term
happiness to people's lives.

How to develop a heart of Compassion

Embrace the Spirit of Compassion

We develop compassion by asking the Almighty God to impart us with the grace or spirit of compassion. Only God has the capacity and power to make us have feelings for others. After all, He has promised to give us a new heart and a new spirit. The Bible says, "A new heart also will I give you, and a new spirit will I put within you: and I will take away the stony heart out of your flesh, and I will give you an heart of flesh." (Ezekiel 36:26)

A stony heart can never show compassion, only the heart of flesh can.

Developing a heart of compassion is possible, if we dare ask God to deposit the caring nature of Jesus in us. Let's sincerely ask the Lord to make us selfless. For selfishness is a robber of compassion. A selfish person cannot really empathise.

Locate a company of compassionate individuals and deliberately associate with them. The fact is that if you find yourself in the midst of compassionate people, the spirit of compassion operating in their lives will rob off on you. Saul found himself in the midst of prophets and he started to prophesy like other prophets. "And when they came thither to the hill, behold, a company of prophets met him; and the

Spirit of God came upon him, and he prophesied among them. And it came to pass, when all that knew him beforetime saw that, behold, he prophesied among the prophets, then the people said one to another, What is this that is come unto the son of Kish? Is Saul also among the prophets?" (1 Sam 10:10-11)

Think Compassion

You become what you think about most often. "For as he thinketh in his heart, so is he..."

(Pro. 23:7)

Decide to expand your heart out to others by developing kind thoughts towards them. Always think about how you can help someone in need. Decide not to get angry or think badly about others.

Engage in Daily Prayers

Pray daily for the hurting people within your family, community and society. The more you pray for people in need the more you develop feelings for them. Pray for orphanages in need of resources and volunteers.

Choose to be Compassionate

God honours our decisions and choices. Develop empathy for your fellow human beings. Once you can empathize with another person, and understand his humanity and suffering, the next step is to want that person to be free from suffering. Choose to put yourself in the shoes of others. Try to imagine the suffering of others as if you are the one going through that suffering. Reflect on how much you would like that suffering to come to an end.

Take Action

Pay a visit to where hurting people are. Visit hospitals, prisons, orphanages and displaced people's camps. You can't visit those places and not be moved with compassion. Many people who visited have been touched to make a difference. As you visit try to give your time and resources toward their well-being. Let hurting or poor people command attention in your budget. Whatever commands priority in your budget is important to your heart. The Bible says, "For where your treasure is, there will your heart be also." (Matthew 6:21)

Beloved, instead of spending lavishly to celebrate your birthday with friends in a flamboyant manner, why not convert that fund to attend to the needs of the poor and less privileged in the society. You will be touching the heart of God by considering the poor. The Bible says, "Blessed is he that considereth the poor: the LORD will deliver him in time of trouble." (Psalms 41:1)

In conclusion, man may forget you! Man may be heartless or viciously compassionless, but God will never forget His children or be heartless toward them! "... for he hath said, I will never leave thee, nor forsake thee." (Heb 13:5)

I pray fervently that God whose compassion is beyond measure; whose compassion is superior to man's, remember you for good as you develop a heart of compassion toward others. And may His rich and abundant blessings be released into your life right now on the basis of His mercy and compassion in Jesus name! "Can a woman forget her sucking child, that she should not have compassion on the son of her womb? yea, they may forget, yet will I not forget thee." (Is. 49:15)

OTHER BOOKS BY THE AUTHOR

Get Motivated! Who says you can't make it?

Hebrew Women's Style

Young but Mighty

Child Neglect: is the Church Guilty

How to Obtain Favour from God and Man

Understanding Courtship and Pre-marital issues

Questions Young People Ask- Vol.1

Essentials of Career Choice

Strategies for Stress free Relationships

Becoming a Celebrated Youth (Youth & Success)

Can Boys and Girls also go to Hell

Teenagers and Relationships

Youth and Friendship

Youth and Opportunity

Striving for Excellence

The Youth God Uses

Building an Effective Youth Ministry

NOTES

NOTES